Also by Nicholas A. Price

Poetry Books

THOUGHTS OF YOU: *AND OTHER LOVE POEMS*

FORGOTTEN HOLIDAY: *AND OTHER POEMS*

BRIDGES TO MANHATTAN: *AND OTHER POETIC JOURNEYS*

Fine Art Photography Books

CLEARED HOT!

PLAYGROUND OF THE GODS

HISTORIC ICONS

For Lily with a view towards the future.

AN ELEPHANT IN MY FRONT YARD

and other observations

by

Nicholas A. Price

A Tough Tribe Book

AN ELPHANT IN MY FRONT YARD: *AND OTHER OBSERVATIONS*
A Tough Tribe Book
Copyright © 2011 Nicholas A. Price

Cover design by S. J. Harris

Cover images and internal illustrations courtesy of Nicholas A. Price ©
2005-2010. All rights reserved

Library of Congress Catalogue in Publication Data on file with the
publisher

First Edition
ISBN 13: 978-0-9798390-2-3
Produced in NEW YORK
Printed and published in the USA
www.ToughTribe.com

OPM 10 9 8 7 6 5 4 3 2 1

TITLE	PAGE

An Elephant in My Front Yard

Heavy eyelid glue exposed
a late night and early morning,
Dysfunctional muscles joining, incessant knocking,
An elephant, in my front yard,
Blanketed sheets, rarely soundproof,
The bed floating, upon a sea of half dreams,
Strawberry and raspberry, sprouting from the lawn,
Sprawling, suffocating, mixed weeds,
Bolted cabbages, steel hard beets,
Hindering hopes of a bountiful harvest,
Carrot and onion fly, continued decimation,
No chance of an escape, only chaos,
The listing mailbox, burdening bills,
My favorite apple tree, shedding weight,
Seething squads, assembled waiting maggots,
Stealing the final wishes, of human exploitation,
Dry pantry cinnamon, dampened,
Ant ranchers, collaborating with acquiescent aphids,
Fluttering whites, establishing hatcheries,
Caterpillar heaven on residual nourishment,
The constant tapping, ceased,
Exchanged for notices posted, threats applied,
I do not want electricity; there is nothing to see,
Suspend the gas, not a thing to cook,
Cut off the water and kill the rest,
It is just another week.

The Jump

Lichen bearded brick and decaying faces overhead,
Stalactites holding on for dearest life,
Directing dirty droplets to earth,
Keep off, no please or politeness,
Shining in officious red and white,
Merging letters meant nothing,
But a posthumous sentence,
Fines unpaid, account closed,
For a moment the world stood still,
Hesitant walkers, stoplight vehicles,
The metallic tapping started,
Strained wire on a tuned instrument,
First distant, then closer,
Oil stained rock, beaten paper, a third line,
Cold afternoon air, always desperate,
Closing early, just like most Wednesdays,
Hardly a deterrent five feet up,
Sixty down into the path,
Hotly burned diesel, fumes spewing,
The one-man show had started,
The performance would soon be over,
A clash of wills as body met steel,
Striking wheels against bright metal,
Reddened rock and rail,
The great engine screeched to a halt,
The driver would never forget.

As Time Slips Through My Hands

Streaming over a craggy descent,
Playful winds whip my enduring hair,
Water boils through river branches,
Once the silky plains of fair skin,
Soft rock heeding to cruel erosion,
Worry and grief, smiles or tears,
I cannot call out stop, suggest another plan,
The road is mapped, the stopwatch started,
A preset course, I am absent from the helm,
No more than just a figurehead,
Without shelter or protection,
Surrendering to the salty sea,
Seared by the severe sun,
The ticking clock travels with the night,
Making up for lost time,
Collecting a little more
from the hourglass empties at my feet,
When the persistent beat is finally silenced,
Judgment will be placed,
Three score and ten, optimistically longer,
As peers and replacements, pass down observations,
A few valiant and others not,
Humble for the three or four, arrogant for ten,
A lover or two will weep, the others applaud,
No more hearts to shatter or embezzle,
The cause of a smile or tear, I can sit and mourn,
Dreaming there is still time for it all,
Plagued by ceaseless hopes and ideas,
Lighting the journey, night and day,
As time slips through my hands.

Deafness

Life had arrived grinding,
At the last halt on the line,
It was Friday again
The day every bored being prays for, the one I hate,
Screeching wheels filling the air,
Proclamations made plain,
One more week, misplaced and masked,
In the growing heap behind me,
Soon I would succumb, to this unstable stack,
Collapsing under the burden
Ready to crash onto my shoulders,
Just as suicidal friends, misplaced forever,
Placed providence in their own hands for a instant,
I never understood why, until today,
Now it was simple,
Everyone could hear them; nobody took time to listen,
Eyes fixed on something else,
Distracted and tuned out,
Yes and okay, just words of dismissal,
The infamous no problem, in reality momentous,
Deafness had infected the masses,
I could not make anyone hear.

Jasmine Terraces

Terraces stacked high with sugary scent,
Spilling murky coffee, miniature cups,
Cobalt and ashen tile tinted, ascending steps,
Scrambling declarations
stated with momentary sincerity,
Glancing down on queen and Carthage,
Conquerors and kings, absurd agendas,
Guarded granite grounds, tumultuous tomes,
Battling books, feuding generations,
Modest knowledge and troubled fabled verses,
Warring hearsay swords, gunned justice,
Jolting the sands of time, plain clay,
Lifeless brains and leaking hearts, readily forgotten,
Marginal viewpoints and a chaotic crowd,
Frenzied storm sweepers, paving destruction,
Radiant possibilities dampened,
Reshaped by silent opposition,
A new day sun festering, a bolted despotic door,
Competent women returned,
Pondering humble homes,
Malodorous troubles beneath,
Sweet scented jasmine terraces.

Life Experience

Your chatter is still audible,
Five feet eleven inches under,
You could never get it right,
I did not believe daisies had six-foot roots either,
Barely scratching the surface,
Yet blighting those lawns of perfection,
Ashes and dust, eternal sand and concrete,
Your only hope of rising, above this deserted creation,
Standing here, looking in at what was,
Hope your chosen naive carriage,
A million blacksmiths could not bend,
This iron rod of destiny,
Hideous heated furnaces, heavy hammer blows,
Our sweat and toil merged into a discontented river,
Buoyed by the rampant rain,
Tempering the solid mass, slippery sludge,
The residence of the ground feeder,
Drowning, they received us
with corrupting open arms,
Summoning us off course,
Entertained by our impossible vision,
The headstrong expectation of wading onward,
Swimming in the open sea of unfettered thoughts,
Middle water, an idle aspiration,
The simple surface, a lifetime of delusion.

Long Gone

When you realize we just might have been right,
Telling you to never hand over the keys,
Allow them to trample on the rights we had fought for,
Giving away the combination to the vault,
Permitting squander and pillage,
Opening your pockets, so that they could refill theirs,
Hiding those ill-gotten gains,
Rewriting the story and telling of our rebellion,
Now you know, it was a struggle for freedom no more,
They took your paid up assets,
Selling them to favored friends, filling their bellies
With the fat of your land, enjoying it somewhere else,
Taking their scissors and mutilating your safety net,
Leaving the children without consideration,
An education teaching them resistance,
Cramming them with fat and a false smile,
A fear of the authority you had dearly paid for,
Filling the given water with putrid residue,
Having theirs delivered in plastic bottles to be sure,

On their rare visits to your world,
Needing more blood, taking their fill,
Departing in leather and walnut,
One day when you walk barefoot,
To what is left of the library,
If they have taught you to read,
Pick up that old and dusty volume,
Forgotten right at the back, marked history,
Turn the pages and actually read,
Not just skim the surface,
You will learn that our predictions were true,
Study those pictures of us, standing on our two feet,
Off to work or on to war, it is just the same,
Look carefully at our struggle,
Determination and resolve,
We had boots on our feet then,
But now we are voiceless and long gone.

Persecuted Poppies

Brushed to the side on the troubled range,
Rotten muddy boot trampled,
Fleeting delicacy falls to the ground,
Joining those in bloodied battle and sullied trench,
Wilting beneath a lottery of rhythmic gunfire,
Reddened earth streams entering foreign soil,
Meadows of mottled carnage, dense disguising weeds,
Open wounds of opiate terror, the same simple flower,
Connected wreaths, solitary remembrance,
Dying for dyed paper and substituted wishes,
Memories forgotten, wavering as time muddies life,
Delivering a harsh message,
The venerable truth of endless conflict,
Tyrants crushed on Flanders fields,
Resurfacing in Farah and further,
The expectation of an era, those bitterly lost souls,
The balance due remains unpaid,
Crushed by an eerie two minute ceasefire,
Unscathed by those rasping tears,
A misplaced generation,
Amid those dimly lit thoughts of desecration,
Chanted wishes from afar,
Falling on rocky resolute ears,
Persecuted poppies, with mercy for no one.

Hidden Graves

They waited until you had breathed your last lungful,
Dismissing the losses, concealing gravelly graves,
Swabbing the stream of flooding tears,
No longer wanting your blotted ballot,
Constructed politics, fashioned breasts,
Opinions harvested, today's caption,
Carrying the brainwashed forward,
Toppling chimneys, jacketing your coal,
Drawing power from every possible punctured lesion,
Openhanded with the keys to your safety net shed,
Wholesale infrastructure and everything left,
Bartering with halfhearted promissory notes,
Coveted cronies, furnished contract orders,
Seizing control, building pointless crossings,
Tipping the garnered gold into deep pockets,
Taking an excessive fill,
Never knowing the flavor of your meager rations.

Wandering Water

Springing into a world without direction,
Taking a hazardous leap,
Meandering through lofty lumber,
Sweetening life on the way,
Inundating the effervescent,
Elaborate woven basin carpets,
Tripping over rigid edges,
Exhausting compliant creases,
Discovering a course across the delicate earth,
Falling for shortcuts, dawdling in luxuriant dells,
Choosing a change of direction,
Throwing oxbows to the fanatical dogs,
As the fishing felines monopolize,
Trapped fins and stifled gills,
Corseted by ditched human desire,
Borrowed for growing wishes,
Hauled to the border for a rest,
Carved away to continue,
Sustaining bulky bucketed coals,
Slick shadowy cargoes,
Displacing channeled venom,
Ugly mouthed industrialized pipes,
Feeding the angling children,
Massacred fish in plastic pails,
Off to an enchanting coastal outing,
Paddling barefoot, in the syrupy brackish surf,
Time to play amongst the wandering water,
Rapidly lost to a majestic lagoon,
Folded along the breaking shore.

Lackluster Hopes

The lethargic landscape rested to the right,
On the left, the wily west whispered wantonly,
Telling of half-truths and winding water,
Forgotten foes, fair-weather friends,
Aching anchorages and slipping ships,
Soulless sailors, broken brothers,
Torrential tides and migrant moisture,
The shifting scenery, solid scenes,
Patchwork painted on a hidden horizon,
Frightened farmers, etching the eager earth,
Daily dreamers, cropped cash,
Clothing children and worrisome woes,
Begging and borrowing,
Waiting for growing green,
Fruitless fertilizer, a doubtful downpour,
The lackluster longing, for greener grass,
A punishing payment for switching sides.

The Topography of Man

The scarifying hands of time,
Sliced cavernous ravines,
Furrows carved,
By the ploughmen of ache and angst,
Light relief in laughing cuts,
Lesser valleys in a fading garden,
Desolation above,
Seismic pinching beneath,
Bottlenecked in time,
Razor respect is blunted further,
Stony features with windswept attrition,
The toll of survival and shifting scenery,
Eyes riveted to an eager past,
Slipping with tapered dreams,
Grasping at an optimistic future,
Cities and streets without mirrors,
Surveying this shifting space,
Redrawing the topography of man.

Unreliable

I am not making an appearance for daylight air today,
The promise of a lingering weekend is over,
Abundant and anonymous, mailbox envelopes stacked,
Endless concertinaed paper, payable yet again,
Postcards home from sociable shores,
Wish you were here,
We will take them next time I am sure,
The notion of a calendar day, another haul,
No need to eat for now, just snooze it away,
Ignore their reluctant engines starting,
Failure a possible pretext, for another day away,
Pouncing on paddling streams, unlocking open fields,
Healthy children and no need for a sick day, or two,
Wildflowers and olive leaves,
The dog had not eaten anything important this time,
Echoing stick forests, sky grabbing reaches and peaks,
No unrepentant deaths, on a bleating Sunday,
Braking for wildlife, not a funeral,
The alarm clock sounds impatiently premature,
Hurried hawks and bushed running rabbits,
The whistling kettle, louder than usual,

Steam excursions and a step backward,
The toaster toasting, perfect toast,
As the sun suffused, sandy beached backs,
The sideboard stacked
with waking coffee and leafy tea,
Stuffed picnic hampers, clean air lunches,
Not a jamming snowy drift or tipping torrential rain,
Tents on the hillside beyond,
An irreversible leaning hurricane force,
Coastal castles, tight wetted sand,
No tsunami wall or vomiting molten shock,
A vaulted oasis, away from the border,
The end of the planet cancelled,
Until the next prediction,
The world war dismissed
the perpetrators apprehended,
Nuclear strategy, packed away
in dusty cardboard boxes,
I have sufficient space to breath,
The world outside is too unreliable.

An Hour in The City

Collected souls clamber through society
Allocated space, mutual mistrust,
Suffering at the curbside of existence,
Crammed into a confining container,
Compositions strained to the end of the dial,
Evading the chill and sweat of survival,
Trumpeting monsters disrupt the rest,
Shambling past, seldom noticing,
Standing close to a parallel plight,
Cat alleys clutch, littered strays,
Utility cage custodians,
Contemporary petroglyphs extend the word,
Deferred decay sprouts from every wall,
Traded for a stony damp cave,
Noise with no volume control,
Pinned to the ramparts of desolation,
Walking carts drift from home,

Cluttering this concrete garden,
Silver and yellow levers litter, just smile and save,
So many cars, fewer wheels, nowhere fast,
City dwellers and clogging brothers,
New metal smog, smoldering fuel,
Clouded haze vaporizes the sunset,
Overlooked by bowed mechanical heads,
Focused on survival and lost pennies,
Driving east or limping north,
Courtesy thrown with discarded wrappers,
Roaming with darkness, homeward bound,
Closing the book on another day,
New chapters, for those remaining clusters,
Gathering in vacated space,
Newborn children, draw a first lungful,
Others break away, on that final journey.

Good Morning

Catapulted from beyond, feeling hardly humorous,
Standing, propped to be precise,
Sprawling hair, rough nocturnal demons,
Hurling it back on my head, from a ninety foot tower,
Visiting dreams, reapplying my skin,
Using the wrong brand of glue,
Absorbing nightmare pillows, every tear swallowed,
Wood shuttered eyes, desiccated cardboard lenses,
Eccentric campers, roping my parched tongue,
Aging travel, geared clocks,
Jaunting through the darkness,
Mustering a merciless marching militia,
Felling fields of stubble growth,
Parting carnage and relentless loss,
Impossible homes, failing cards,
Scattered fading gardens, rime bitten life,
A chill night of ugly heads, snowy teeth,
The dog whistle calling, two hundred and twelve,
Navigating ear to ear, a tender head,
Everything mislaid in between,
Caffeine shepherds, round up the latest day,
Time again, for good a morning, that never was.

Paddling

I visited the future today,
Seeing those uncomplicated children,
Paddling on the shore,
Wet, cold and entertained,
Engaging gulls, tricky to ensnare,
Ceaseless breakers, despite my absence,
Wondering if they rested, when I went home,
Shelled disorder floored at my feet,
Joining the mass of stranded predecessors,
Onshore breezes sending relief,
Putrid pollution back to the land,
Surf workers, up and down,
Feathered mass transit,
Suddenly someone selfish stole the sun,
Raised a diminutive new moon,
Darkness draped a blanketed panorama,
Shivering realization started,
The endless beach debriefing,
Sand everywhere,
In every quivering crevice, it had legs,
The saline air, ushering sleepy sentiment,
Time to go home,
Journeying back to the past.

Change?

Optimistically you smiled,
Telling of how, everything had changed,
Careless dragged me into the Balkan air,
Eagerly awaiting a new world,
Old Crusty taking over,
Dipping in to pothole fields,
Guided by western contributions,
Unstable landing seats, stuffed streets, frigid waste,
Home heating suspended,
The heart of an unhappy winter,
Every line, longer than before,
Rowed dark figures in wintered coats,
Elderly and unfortunate, older and poorer,
The unsanctioned rich, loaded with a pungent tang,
Recently printed, sequential dollar bills,
Every other note, handed over fists full of nothing,
Foreign paper for bread and soup,
Warm water courtesy of sleeping lava,
Sad surface fires raging,
Clockwork buses dodging the melt,
Weary worn shoes stepping, clods of gray compaction,
Carefully caged, rolling past in oblivion,
Your newly engineered, imported machine,
Change was tremendous, but not for the rest,
Age-old sufferance, harnessed to a future runner,
Misplaced gray effigies of another time,
Toppled awaiting collection, austere facades,
Softened by a simple white weather layer,
Glinting red stars passing,
Quickly stolen away for cautious concealment,
The dread of resurrection and an end to change.

A World Without Mathematics

The mathematician scratched his balding head,
The kind that regularly overheats,
Right in the middle, with the center of activity,
The rest of his remaining hair, a pristine garden hedge,
The kind that fanatic gardeners attend to daily,
No crafted patterns, the shapes of ducks,
Cones of other bizarre additions,
Nevertheless, extremely well clipped,
The reason for the troubled scratching,
Not the usual outlandish equation,
The kind that had left you wishing,
I can surely spell algebra;
I just wish I had learned its application,
It was the breaking news,
The government had decided, in its wisdom as always,
To abolish mathematics,
Improving their chances at the polls,

No more troubling trade figure explanations,
No adding up the unemployed,
Counting the bothersome opposition votes,
Majority and minority would be no longer,
A percentage point away from trouble,
Deficits outdated,
The scratching ceased,
Reaching for a sheet of plain white paper,
Lifting his worn down pencil and twelve inch ruler,
He appeared prepared to write a lengthy complaint,
But not dear sir or madam,
Darling government please be reasonable,
He took the ruler to the edge
and rapidly scribbled a note,
Length multiplied by breadth,
Equals the square area of the subject in hand.

Another Map

I never want to see another map,
Fenced and broken borders, moving pain,
Drawing territory on a patchy planet,
Striking fabric layers,
Warp and weft suspiciously confronted,
Lines of right and wrong,
Wealthy rows, poverty slides,
Warring factions and peaceful parties,
Lovers of freedom and haters of liberty,
A fiefdom of immigrants, emigrating,
Across a graphic globe,
Flouting the flow of the water,
Severing the sides of lonely peaks,
Bridging bountiful valleys,
Sketching in the sea,
Infinite ocean adventures,
Counting and labeling us all,
Debris and long shore drift,
Contempt and hope,
Trampled into the same sand,
Leaving a set of divisive geographical accounts,
Unfolded and pinned to an officious wall,
Lost chances of universal opportunity.

Now You Are Dead

Now you are dead I think of you more,
Mostly out of pity and a life half lived,
I no longer have to call,
As if it was some dutiful act,
We no longer have to lie,
Discuss how good things are,
I no longer have to visit,
Long silences and never knowing what to say,
I no longer have to see you,
Deteriorating in front of my eyes,
I no longer have to make polite conversation,
For fear of being out of your league,
We no longer have to look back,
Upon those times, supposedly better,
I no longer have to think about charity,
I understand, pride is always painful,
I no longer have to inhale,
Your whisky and cigarette coated breath,
We no longer have to advise,
Each other, in any way,
I no longer have to tolerate,
Your insufferable wife,
I no longer have to hear your great plans,
I never have time enough for my own,
Now you are dead and in my thoughts,
I have you neatly compartmentalized somewhere,
I imagine you interfering with roots,
Fending off maggots with some new invention.

Rain Today

I yearn for a downpour today,
Hearing that heavy untapped inundation,
Sitting and reading the news,
In front of this obscured pane,
Swabbing torrents and misplaced gutters,
Hiding the earth from drained eyes,
Every story will be a work of fiction,
As the drizzled glass conceals the pain,
Streaming distant headlights,
Part of a meandering river,
Sporadic blue and red, flowers on the rise,
Recently excavated graves, ponds for new life,
Headstone rows; garden sculptures,
Sullied secrets and corrupt causes,
Flowing downstream with memories,
Diluting the polluted acidic skies,
Quenching the thirst stricken fields,
I wish it would rain forever.

The Ants of Alang

Teasing the wharf side ropes,
Thoughts of escape for the last time,
No master to make the call,
An expedition to the edge,
Building on the copiously caked layers,
Succumbing to the salted depths of decay,
The ants of Alang would soon scrabble,
Over her weary carrion corpse,
From bow to aft with merciless hammers,
Scorching her heart, scolding torches,
Port and starboard machined and reworked,
Soon to be, a simple static, washer or dryer,
The robust stern stripped and reduced,
New silver and shaving shards,
Razor reefers and rough driven decks,
Wheeled away, rolled, beaten and fired,
Beams and drilled bolted bars,
Fairings headed for fixing fasteners,
Lofty spars and spoons,
Proud forecastles to toy castles,
Masts into maquettes,
Waste to the wind, oil to the ocean,
Dropped with a high tide,
Broken on the beach, without bathers.

The Lodgings

Weekly rent and weakly lit,
Dismal corridors hold the collective scent,
Efficiently hoarded souls,
Boxed claustrophobia on moist frigid air,
Blending the catering scent of every ethnicity,
Soaking the sound from each station,
Humor to horror, infinite news,
Insipid commercials with numbers to call,
Thumping melodies, old and new,
Banality spewing under every door,
Reluctant stair climbers, second, third and forth,
Lowered heads in attic space,
Pasted metal numbers,
Watching poorly painted floors,
Abundant locks, endless precut keys,
Temporary with the tenants,
Patched forced entry, week to week,
Rough handed and weathered,
Effortless targets, accurate arms,
Any disturbance ignored,
Doubtless well aware, above and below,
Furtively increasing the volume control,
Warranting later claims of nothing heard,
Tripped on the first flight down,
Assisted with a push, no stopping,
Cracked and compressed into this decaying dive,
A home for suspects, not humans,
Living in the lodgings, a temporary option.

Heldorado Days

I had never heard of Heldorado Day,
Even though I had experienced hell,
In the incessant heat of desert hikes,
I remembered the lawyer walking to the temple,
Suit and trainers, no formal shoes,
Comfortable for those roasting streets,
Today was no different, heading the parade,
Not the sadness and humble pride of Veterans Day,
Beloved warriors and those that never returned,
Everyone approached together,
As if they had just stepped off
Mayflower decks, with simple threadbare luggage,
A world of promise,
The boulevard smiled from end to end,
Longer shadows, not in life but on the street,
Midday in the developed desert,
Grinning cops and cowboys,
Nineteen fifties beauty queens,
Husbands from the thirties,
Parents from south of the border,
Children born a few miles from here,
Fighting thirst, shading umbrellas,
All one and undivided, snaking with the parade.

Off to a Better Place

So glad to hear, you are off to a better place,
Tell me more about it, my hesitation is simple,
I just hope the messenger had visited first hand to see,
Remember that politician friend of yours,
He told you how you had never had it so good,
Remember the singer you liked,
The one who sung about, how wonderful life was,
The day you fell for the girl of your dreams,
You were head over heels in love with her,
She told you that her love would last forever,
The month before she married your best friend,
I remember when I visited you in hospital,
Yes, the third time that is,
The day your brother told you it was safe,
Before you jumped, I never trusted him either,
Your grandfather was no better,
Telling you how he was in the army too,
Surviving two wars without a scratch,
The day you cycled to the barracks
and that bus hit you,
I believe you are right; the driver did not look twice,
Personally, I do not think he looked once,
I had never seen an enemy combatant undercover,
Especially as a bus driver, until that day,

Transport and you have never really gelled,
The time your mother convinced you,
Flying was dangerous,
I agree, it was unusual for that ship to sink
in such fine weather,
You looked quite different when you returned,
Thirty days at sea in a life raft with no food or a razor,
Consider the time the doctor told you
everything will be okay,
When he started the saw,
I knew he could not tell his right from left,
It did make chasing the nurses a challenge,
I thought the cut of your stockbrokers suit was sharper,
That one he wore to court,
On the day of his sentencing, twenty years,
The judge was not impressed with embezzlement,
It is a good thing the hospital paid you compensation,
As you could not afford to pay them,
Now I reflect upon your life,
Considering those ups, mostly downs,
Maybe that is why someone said;
you are off to a better place,
Frankly, it could not be any worse, could it?

Questions on The Edge

Did she take pleasure in seeing us out on the edge?
Wanting to gain his fading attention,
I do not remember it waning,
Biting our nails without seatbelts,
Wondering of the outcome,
Whether we would be thrown from the car,
Make it as far as that clinical smell,
Perhaps she had succeeded this time,
We would not be collecting her,
No further excuses for her absence,
Fat lies, conveniently filed under the ugly truth,
The end of a deceptive conspiracy,
This time it would be the coroner on call,
The doctor could treat those other sick people,
With broken legs and inflated bowels
Pain that never parted, patients wanting to live,
Having bumped into something unforeseen,
Bottles of pills consumed over time,
For illness and ache,
Not in one afternoon, with a jug of gin
and a fading ultimatum,
We would be left to continue,
Paint over those pink bedroom walls,
Send all her clothes to a charity shop,
Left living on almost burnt toast,
With something on top,
His only culinary contribution.

Broken Promises

The apparition unfurls,
Loosened pages and rusted staples,
Crossed out and underlined,
Characters in every margin,
The wrong side of the tracks,
Simple rows of tattered shacks,
Plainly etched hypocrisy, grows with every hedge,
Clammy cardboard heaped high,
Bursting with broken promises and yesterday's news,
Carpeting the floor with every pledge of change,
Rising profits roaming, on the back of degradation,
Scaling damp travels,
At the pace of political aspiration,
Sparing no one from those lofty ideals,
No sturdy legs support this giddy mushroom,
Just an empty store,
Once overflowing with stock,
Heartless hopes in muted reflections,
Framed with a mold tainted mirror,
Partially illuminated, badly boarded,
Renovation on hold,
Punctual freight, obstructs the path,
Spreading decibel messages,
Along a mile of graffiti splashed trucks,
Billboards on the move,
Obscuring your view of the dream.

Thank you Father

Thank you father, for the aide memoire,
You spoke of a blemish, on the backside of society,
I never heeded your opinion, as I watched helplessly,
They ground you into the earth,
Extracting your life blood,
Under a tyrannical thumb force,
Bleeding you for taxed devotion,
Waving your counted flag,
Welded to the wall of the nation,
Newspapers bleating odds,
Sheepish news and political prejudice,
Unfurling rich guarantees in your deepest seas,
Entertained by the state,
As they trapped your treasures,
Sprinting for some sunlit southern shore,
Leaving you shoveling the sour snows of winter,
Paving a path towards your dreary dwelling,
In some supposedly sheltered suburb,
Struggling with a frozen carriage,

Reeking of rot and carpeted use,
With a blinking eye they would come knocking,
If required, breaking down your door,
Searching for a final hidden coin,
A murky magazine, not scrutinized by the censors,
Broadcasters and receivers, required compensation,
A two sided smile, exchanged for your tallied vote,
Throwing authority in the path of dignity,
Promising you the assistance required,
They lied,
Handing it all, to the first person through the door,
I watched you wallow,
In the land you loved and tolerated,
Convinced and blinded by a mountainous deception,
Unable to converse with your brainwashed soul,
I climbed aboard the last plane leaving,
Thank you Father,
Please switch off the lights.

The Bucolic Backwater

You could never see over the hill,
Effortlessly keeping you from wandering,
Seeing the other side, bursting with immorality,
A chance of deserting, the bucolic backwater,
Persuading you the world was flat,
Easy to plow that way,
Until you dropped off the edge,
Setting your aching back
and strained heart into the land,
For a paltry penny and a potato or two,
Fenced in with the farmyard,
Flora and fauna, suffering continual husbandry,
Until ritual slaughter,
Trucking in the needs, imported from hell,
The other world,
Where every soul slaved, in searing flames,
Burning to death to pass you beaten metal,
Fashioning contours in the tools you desire,
Rotating the loam, gratifying the idle birds,
Paying your debts,
With the bloody carcasses of hard labor,
Appeasing the incessant craving for more,
Holding your head bowed in terror,
Never looking up to ask why,
The sun always sets on the other side.

Washed Out

The jagged downpour dropped,
The grime of endless stale days,
Muddying my evergreen optimism,
Pausing every promising prospect,
Saturating the simple plantings,
Drowning those earthen seeded souls,
Tipping fertility downstream,
Away from a garden dream,
Herbal flavors shifting, a clinical culinary collision,
Lavender and rosemary, wrapping the putrid air,
Streaming off,
To barren lands of drained transient time,
Where germinating children, etch an existence,
Waiting for a sun scorched tomorrow,
Delivering a deliberate drying death,
Upon a lame land, nourishing worthless weeds,
Slaughtering every horticultural hope,
My blossoming prizefighters competing,
With the monotonous compacted turf,
The picketed posts and paved parking plots,
Halted in a dream quest,
Shattering the mowed maze,
Stamping color on a dull palette.

The Bitter End

The dial rotated, for the last time,
The same profound steel wire,
Plummeting nine thousand times before,
Into a supported, temporary world,
Breaking for Sunday safeguards,
A seaside holiday or two,
A hospital visit and four funerals,
A rapid dose of winter flu,
Descending blue, emerging black
Winded with sulfurous damp dark dust,
Sporadic dirty downpours, no umbrella,
Sturdy for an age in unity,
Crashing divided, never burning,
Naked hands grappling,
One hundred truncheon centers,
Trodden under foot,
Loaded into eager transport,
Loyal thousands overlooked,
Six months handed down,
Shielding theirs, beaten to the bitter end,
Left packed on the cold surface,
Pain is paid off, wrongs never righted,
Suffocating black powder, disappointment,
Enduring challengers, consuming their words,
New world shovels fulfilling the call,
Setting their tables,
Mothballing your world,
Hidden from scrutiny, well below ground level.

.

Sickness

It was a difficult day,
A carefully disguised spy, selling malware,
Rode into my life,
On the back of an ailing Trojan horse,
Transporting an infectious virus,
The steed had devoured a crate of carrots,
Full of worms,
The poor contaminated creature was infected,
I soon learnt of my inadequacies,
The firewall I had so carefully constructed around me,
Was effortlessly perforated,
I called my expert neighbor,
However, he was out tracking cookies,
The only other person I could call,
Was on a phishing holiday,
I picked up my telephone,
A desperate attempt to summon assistance,
I soon learned, I had eaten every minute in my quota,
Quarantine would be the only answer.

Cemetery Road

Just a visitor today,
Ambling along with the organized lime path,
The final journey for the interns,
Precisely set, row upon row,
Final statements chased in stone,
Chosen as a rule by others,
No space for the conceptual,
Breathing room for eccentricity,
Huddled as in life,
Commuters in death,
Standing in line,
Ready to board some crowded train,
Searching for a seat,
Packed buses on a drizzling day,
Carefully arranged,
Interrupted in this afterworld,
Hard cash prevails,
Funding those sporadic skyscrapers,
Emerging from the masses,

Above the ordinary suburban stump,
Proclaiming I was, look at me!
Pointless pink marble,
Over the somber gray and obsidian black,
Spaces with just a marker,
Flowers for a year, perhaps two,
Soon there is so much else to do,
Invading life lifts from the nourished earth,
Plaguing the inscriptions,
Softening the masons handed edge,
Hiding the trite sympathetic sentences,
From those left behind,
Waiting for autumn leaves,
Landing at will,
Abstract and anonymous,
Forsaken for a while,
Hiding beneath the cloaking winter,
Until remembrance returns,
With the gentle buds of spring.

Progress

Is it you, this grief I feel,
The loss of Americana for me
My weary eyes shift to sadness,
With the light speed of change,
Dread is on the face of every passenger,
Crushing surges and whitewashed wills,
Heartbreaking hope keeping pace,
Am I in this loop or are you passing me by,
Racing through the mysterious night,
Darkness hours, no longer mine,
Slithering away, my grasp weakens,
Powerless to hamper your march,
Firmly clasping the revolutionary tracks,
Advancing alone with stony new faces,
I am forgotten,
Just one more voice in the middle crowd,
Obscured by the sound of intensity,
Forging progress on the latest shiny anvils,
Pioneers swept up in your wake,
Securing ashes and bones, the foundations,
Trickling veins lubricating, overheated machines,
Sweat and tears quenching an undying thirst,

Transformation is the only future,
The invitations are always mailed first class,
Appealing for new blood,
Departing those historical wastelands,
Industrial hubs join the wheeled ghosts,
Of an ancient era,
History replicates the hidden age,
Titanic dinosaurs, dormant and silently waiting,
For an appointment with the torch,
Fragmented metal and evocative oil, all that remains,
Saturating a once productive earth,
Now they are the vendors, tickets to a fresh show,
In the desiccated territory of bright hope,
Promised western daydreams and sticky opportunities,
Master plans fusing with major wishes,
You pass on by,
Leaving me in the roadside dust,
With a lonely love for Americana.

Lost Sheep

The path of unknowing martyrs,
Blocked from the festivities,
Saved from the holy knife, butchery on hold,
Fresh obstacles and parallel palm puzzles,
Muddling the passage across the sand,
Boxed bungalows for new arrivals,
Floral prints and littered land,
Roadway routes, Berbers in rags,
New obstructions, for tired feet,
Better placed in unlocked land,
The penny pinching emporiums,
Gripping territorial corners,
New passageways, conveyed customers,
Directed towards a ritualistic fleecing,
Feasting daily, birthdays once a year,
Fasting amid snacks, longer durations,
Disrupted profit,
Inquisitive famished waiters,
Pondering the possibility of a rapidly setting sun,
Four wheels and no humped carriages,
Trailing fennel heaps and earthen truffles,
Rams arriving head to head,
Meetings with bleating lost sheep.

The Old Guard

Swathed in dutiful ribbons,
Carrying pride and compassion,
Dropped like searing coal, into a pool of tepid water,
Indifferent youthful views, freedom and dreams,
Overstuffed and disillusioned, on a four square block,
Opinions floating with the debris,
Hearsay of the daily tide,
Commenting without comprehension,
Aimless outlooks,
Attacking at arm's length, untouched by your losses,
Those tired fingers tipped,
With a brother's burgundy blood,
Flowing freely, covering your empathetic offerings,
Those broken frames and planted wounded fields,
Now, old foes fuel, the oiled production lines,
Extracting dream drops from industrial influence,
Whilst first-class friends, part ways forever,
Holding on to the fragments of embossed metal,
Exchanging a dusty reward, for seven tenths of a life,
Leaving and taking those well-thumbed volumes,
An extensive library of checks and balances,
Lifting the anchors, once steadying a troubled ship,
Soon the cynics discover you never held us back,
You continued to hold us together.

Nightfall on The Water

Struggle strolled across the streams,
Downhearted spirit damsels darting,
Water to earth, earth to water,
The looming past records, never straight,
The unheard voices, forever exploited,
Suffering laid down and forgotten,
Restless and rolling,
Murmuring into the still ether,
Their claustrophobic ache,
Entombed in a bottomless grave,
Hard running nightmares,
Dying with the dawn,
Drowning in the oblivion,
False freedom tenders,
Disappearing with a detached sun,
Where few are fated, the rest remain,
Continuing to fall for a misplaced cause,
Flowing blood rippling, on an endless surface,
Lost in the landing sea of a perpetual night.

Existence

A lost tree muscling for space,
In a blending forest evergreen,
Stationary and waiting, lightning fires,
Bending hurricane gusts, wilting acid rain,
Aching from antlers and gnawing rodents,
Hacking firewood hunters,
Those night carving lovers,
Soon at the hands of the lumber cutter,
There would be pain and with it release,
Escape from this sleepy land of fixed parameters,
The main mast of a tall ship,
Heading into the arms of the open sea.

Running Away

Today I ran away with big top dreams,
In town for a few days, pitched on temporary turf,
Coupled camels, two-foot ropes on stadium stands,
Desultory domestics, corralled upon a quarter,
Nimble shoed hoofs trot the grave asphalt,
Itinerant elephants find a concretized forest,
Beneath those ancient feet, fearing a silvery hook,
Shading from a stationary sun, ready to run the ring,
The morning after,
Performing people lose their foundation,
Hanging cooperative costumes,
In humble wheeled homes,
Stacking and stuffing, sugary delights,
Jesters weighting the burdening tent,
Foolish accidents, no applause today,
The ringmaster, no topper and tails,
Saggy slacks and foldaway seating,
Voiceless and sweating, the strain of moving on,
Breaking down and putting up,
Magic moves and falls,
Ready for a fresh circle and anticipated laughter,
Galloping horses, dancing dogs,
Inflated prices and helium balloons,
Taming the trapped monsters,
As night bodies float, in the warm netted air,
Ten years of trepidation, two minutes of shock,
Tomorrow, I am leaving the circus.

The Earthen Void

Stark stockades with perpendicular purpose,
Emerge from the crust,
Climbing daily, obstructing observation,
Blotted lavish landscapes,
Inky blue, ocean views,
Prying with peaks and surging terrain,
Seeking a confrontation with simple clouds,
Throwing down a shadowy proclamation,
Pompous prowess towards the earth,
Concrete obelisks illuminating the sky,
Slaughtering stars,
Sandwiched velvet and divided trees,
Fissure follies,
Strung together with sieved wire and tacky tar,
Leaching into the contiguous earth,
Running for ruined rivers,
Infecting the ether,
Fatal fumes of flaming force,
Cat people,
Hunting for one, sleeping twenty-three,
Modest boxes stream with space traveling harvests,
Packed and sliced, fleshy liaisons,
Washed with auburn liquids,
Sucked from foreign fields,
The diminutive fish waiting,
Constrained by ever-smaller cans.

Yesterday's News

Yesterday's news is now bedding,
Capital accounts and stock market listings,
Economic paper, sheets and blankets for some,
Yesterday's box is a home,
Yesterday's soda brings profit,
With no chance of a listing,
Where cash is the king, for those without cards,
Income is scarce, sustenance required,
On the top floor and in the doorway,
Despised and stepped over,
A forgotten exile, alone and unaided,
Fending for a borrowed plot,
Erected cardboard spaces and life itself,
Society has turned its back, a reluctant sponsor,
Blinded, deaf and dumb,
You have become, yesterday's news.

The Hunt

Frivolous faces had me floundering,
Captivated by a lack of clemency,
Thrown to the crowded banks,
Dropped from the ashen roofs,
Grounded with acorn roots, by the hunting party,
Pressed out of my lair by new money,
Ruddy faces reddened with aristocratic coats,
Inebriated fools and oversized foals,
Plaguing dogs and a bitter daybreak pursuit,
Frozen foot fields,
Hampered hopes of autumnal leaves,
Strong summer wings and springing promise,
Down to the discontented depths of fever gauges,
Thickening fingers, claw bitten birch bark,
Lung signals painted on the airy dew,
Crisp green gripping the lessening boughs,
Hurried heather on headland hopes,
Cold whittled nettles and frost bitten dock,
Out in the open, a blood drained skull,
Feathery thoughts and weighty pads,
Beaten and shredded for historic pleasure.

Gas Flaming and Taxis

No wild cat safari with sightseeing dreamers,
Elephant streets,
Booming and busting with wildebeest,
Just the stench of bodies, mile high stacked,
Gas flaming and taxis going nowhere fast,
Plump influence, lean puppet children,
Drawing the endless black gold,
Sifting ancient sand, for polished promise,
Delivering poverty and dispossessed souls,
A larder packed with malnutrition,
Controlling the reigns,
Invited aliens are the feasting guests at your table,
Their allies dispatched, naming safety and security,
Cutting them down in showers of poison lead,
Taxing the corpses,
Gifting gilded coats to the chosen few,
Education and health, luxuries of a decadent world,
Idealism, one persons dream,
This week's custodian,
Advertising your ancestral gems,
Drip fed payments, no fair deal,
Crushed votes and established control,
Another contracted gift, more than you ever need,
Where does all that green paper go?
Ten big cars and a dozen wives,
Far from this impotent stench,
Mansions strewn across a liberated planet,
Leaving the dissenters, no trial,
Hanging from hempen rope,
A pilfered peninsula, hemorrhaging oil.

Winter

In from oblivion, leaving your hidden void,
The time is yours,
Stealing my cerulean skies with steel gray eyes,
Marshalling my affectionate sun,
To some far-off place,
Illuminating days, open radiance,
Precious flames, curbing darkness,
Frozen naked in a bitter draught,
Robbed of those embracing, gentle rays,
Pitching icing fingers,
Flinging me to the dogs of zero and below,
Vulnerable flesh, ruthlessly bitten,
Carting away the warmth, quiescent in my bones,
Parting with a chill, once yours,
Dropping me swiftly, on to the next victim,
Leaving a discontented lost trail,
Brush whitening leafy path trees,
Destroying the last promised life,
Set on a wounding course,
Suffocating the last of my living color,
Blanketing the variants, friendly textures,
Carrying bitter gloom upon your shoulders,
Hopelessly holding on for spring.

The Inner Sanctum

The final seals applied, tightly bolted,
Claustrophobic calls and boundless clatter,
Continual processing, information absorbed,
Witnessing these endless fragments,
Breaching and muddling rarified air,
Butchery, ecstasy and adoration,
Stirred in the same tarnished trough,
Shadow chambers, steadfast protection
Nowhere to hide,
Tungsten bars, dead bolted,
Humble locksmiths lost, no keys,
Detainees with life sentences,
Awaiting the liberating penalty,
An abrupt route to freedom,
The ticking red clock, echoes time,
Soon a burning obsession,
Tallying every second in each minute,
Haunted by a past we cannot transform,
Horrified by the present,
Suspicious of the next bend,
Those pessimistic plans for tomorrow,
Fixated on a future, we know little about,
Cruelly confined to the inner sanctum.

Feeding Time

Capturing the sullied ache, a fruitless picture,
Huddled and humble, fenced drab statues,
Sleeping bag homes and shopping cart lives,
Grocery sack suitcases, portable possessions,
Downhill recycling, crossroad rows,
Daily dinner, the solitary salvation,
From blazing heat and melting tar,
Pavement homes and barren bulwarks,
Walkway windows and living plots,
Transitory wheels with eyes forward,
Slipping the line, expanding each day,
A queue of mourners, grieving life lost,
Eighty years old and eight months young,
Escaping a fracture in civilization,
Cigarette currency and bartered space,
Washing machines and a cold shower,
Daily dirt escapades, barred soap,
In a flood channel with no rain,
Last year's bodies downstream,
Feeding time at Foremaster Lane.

Blood Oranges and Foreign Fields

It had been another despotic week,
Five stars and bugs, even on the seventh floor,
Not a single beautiful woman, dipping in the pool,
Just endless meetings with regime people,
My suggestions, raising eyebrows,
Locking up the opposition is undemocratic,
Off to restless fields and recently plowed clay,
Apparently abandoned corrugated shacks,
The orange groves in close proximity,
Mere agricultural dreams of simple people,
Cultivated for me or some deeper hole,
Ready for fennel seeds and poppy strays,
My telephone was an airport hostage,
It probably would not work, in this wilderness,
Who could I call anyway,
Out of contact with the world I knew,
I was looking for shovels and lime,
Gone with the cabbages and carrots,
Fertilizer and famished maggots.

The Drummer

The drummer played on,
Beating the taught skin of earth,
With the hardwood sticks of life,
Watching survivors, cling desperately,
Some were lucky, holding close to the edge,
Huddling in crowded cities,
False security, never venturing far,
Marred by the ubiquitous tainted rhythm,
Hindering their dreams,
Heads down and involved,
Ignorant of change,
Subsistence the only goal,
Costly results for the risk takers,
Altering the metronome of habitation,
Revolutionaries in status quo,
Forever moved, in tune with a new pace,
Breaking away from surface pain,
Funerals and rebirth engineering,
Futile escapes, the tempo set in stone,
The drummer played on.

The Weight

The cruel weight of the world grew heavier,
Daily heaped upon my shoulders,
The woes of the earth,
Broad perhaps, hauling this burden,
Smoldering with the ashes of war,
Tormented by life and the death of innocence,
Every outlook stifled by a continual storm,
Deafened by the wheels of confusion,
Scalded by fiery injustice,
Slaughtered infants and blinkered judges,
Theft goes punished,
With frequently collared dogs,
Permits to massacre, exchanged for ready money,
Tyranny bought more,
Experiments started, never concluded,
Children throwing aside yesterdays toys,
Demanding new,
Bread and water arrived at a dreadful cost,
Life measured, against bullion bars,
Bartering buried out of sight,
The human race, herded into clusters,
No calculation brought equality,
The load was too much to bear
I rolled the incredible globe off my conscience,
Not another soul seemed to care.

ABOUT THE AUTHOR

Nicholas Price is a poet whose work has been published through a series of bespoke and mainstream publications and books.

With a legacy of work now collated and published in several new titles, bringing a unique poetic style and perspective to a wide range of subjects enjoyed by all readers and ages.

His poetry, writings and photographic work have been exhibited at key events and institutions. The acclaimed collection titled *Cleared Hot!* – a photographic story and essay - was acquired by one of the world's most prestigious institutions, the United States Library of Congress.

OTHER AVAILABLE TITLES

BRIDGES TO MANHATTAN
and other poetic journeys

Nicholas A. Price

America is a way of life and a state of mind, to be savored and discovered.
Nicholas Price celebrates this beauty and diversity through his poetic artistry. His journeys take us from the Bridges to Manhattan to the pioneer trails of the West Coast and beyond.

Nicholas Price takes us on a poetic journey through childhood and life experience.

Nostalgic, amusing and a must read for those who sometimes question; "whatever happened to the world we grew up in?"

Forgotten Holiday is one book to keep amongst your own treasure trove of memories.

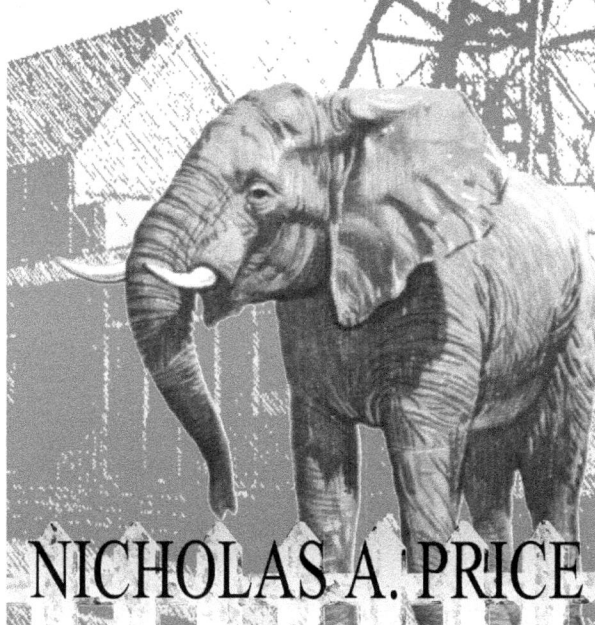

an ELEPHANT
IN MY FRONT YARD
and other observations

NICHOLAS A. PRICE

Nicholas Price presents his frank and sometimes humorous poetic
thoughts and observations on life.
From social and political change to the hopes of us all.

Described as "a refreshing new voice in poetry", these works are
timeless and reflective of the world we once knew and the one we
have become.

Thoughts of You
and other love poems

Nicholas A. Price

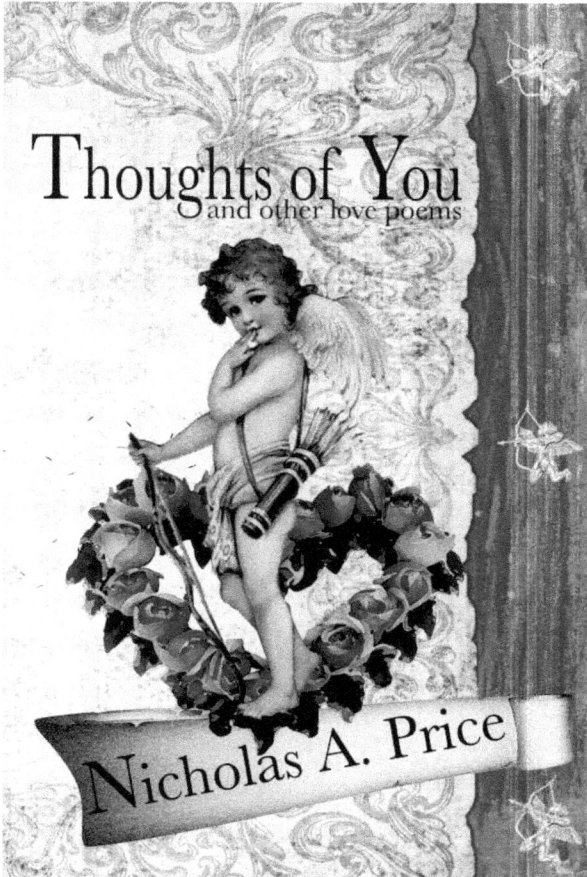

How would you describe being in love to someone who has never
experienced it?
Poet Nicholas Price pens the human storms of desire, heartbreak
and devotion.
The distant yearning to unyielding passion, absence and
infidelity, grief and solitude, those erratic and chaotic emotions
we call love.

Tough Tribe

ToughTribe.com

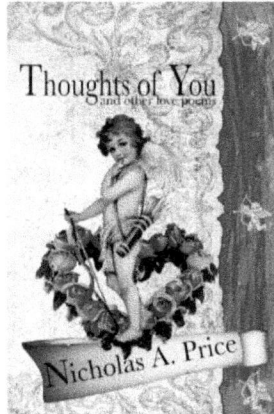

Buy All Four Books
At Our Special Collector Set Price

www.ToughTribe.com
Also available at Amazon.com and all other fine bookstores

www.ingramcontent.com/pod-product-compliance
Lightning Source LLC
LaVergne TN
LVHW021351080426
835508LV00020B/2234